WHAT · DO · WE · KNOW

ABOUT  THE

ROMANS · ?

MIKE · CORBISHLEY

PETER BEDRICK BOOKS
NEW YORK

Published by
Peter Bedrick Books
2112 Broadway
New York, NY 10023
Text © Mike Corbishley 1991
Illustration © Simon & Schuster Young Books 1991

Library of Congress Cataloging-in-Publication Data
Corbishley, Mike.
   What do we know about the Romans?/Mike Corbishley. – 1st American ed.
   Includes index.
   Summary: An illustrated survey of the history, people, and everyday life in ancient Rome.
   ISBN 0–87226–352–5
   1. Rome – Civilization – Juvenile literature. [1. Rome – Civilization.]   I. Title.
   DG77.C593   1992
937 – dc20   91–28763
                                                                                    CIP
                                                                                    AC

Design: David West
           Children's Book Design
Illustrator: Rob Shone
Copy editor: Ros Mair
Picture research: Jennie Karrach

Photograph acknowledgements:
The Ancient Art & Architecture Collection: Cover, 8, 12–13 (below), 16, 17, 20, 22 (below), 25, 26, 29, 32–33 (below), 34; The Trustees of the British Museum: 31; Mike Corbishley: 19 (below), 28 (below); C.M. Dixon: endpages, 9, 14, 19 (above), 22 (above), 23 30, 37, 38, 39, 40–41, 41, 42 (both); Werner Forman Archive: 18, 32, Naples Museum: 21; The Grosvenor Museum, Chester: 31; Sonia Halliday Photos: 13, 28, 35 (above); Michael Holford: 9, 21, 24, 26, 27, 39, 40; National Museum of Wales: 43
Cover: Portrait of a man and wife, Pompeii

Typeset by: Goodfellow & Egan, Cambridge. *Printed and bound in* Hong Kong
Second printing 1995

· CONTENTS ·

WHO·WERE ·THE· ROMANS?

Look at the map on this page. The dotted lines show the area the Romans occupied between AD 100 and 200. They called all this land their empire. About 60 million people lived inside the frontiers of the empire. But it had not always been like this. The Romans originally came from the area close to Rome. This tribe, called the *Latins*, gradually conquered all the other tribes around and pushed their frontiers out into the rest of Italy. They were good at fighting and organization. Eventually they even defeated the powerful Carthaginians.

A BANQUET SCENE
No single picture can capture the image of a typical ordinary Roman man or woman. So many people from so many different lands and backgrounds formed the Roman population. This piece of sculpture (a painted carving in stone) shows a scene at a banquet for rich people. The guests are wearing the sort of clothes worn by the wealthiest Romans. You can find out more about what they are wearing and what they might be eating further on in this book (see pages 12–15 and 26–27).

BRITANNIA

Londinium

GERMANIA INFERIOR

BELGICA

LUGDUNENSIS GALLIA

ATLANTIC OCEAN

GERMAN SUPERIC

ACQUITANIA

POENINAE ALPES

ALPES COTTAIE

NARBONENSIS

ALPE MARITIM

CORSICA

TARRACONENSIS

LUSITANIA

SARDINIA

BAETICA

Carthago

MAURETANIA TINGITANA

MAURETANIA CAESARIENSIS

AFRI

A ROMAN SOLDIER AND HIS WIFE

How can we know what Roman people looked like? Some people had their likenesses carved onto their tombstones. This soldier and his wife lived in a Roman town called Nemausus (Nîmes) in the southernmost part of the great Roman province of Gaul (now France).

A PORTRAIT FROM EGYPT

This lifelike portrait of a bearded man was painted onto a wooden panel that was placed over his mummified body when it was buried in Egypt. He was a Roman Priest of the Sun God, which is why he wears a star on his forehead.

 LANGUAGE

Latin was the language spoken by the earliest Romans – the Latins. It became the official language of the empire, although many conquered peoples went on speaking their own language. Because the Roman Empire spread so far around the world, a lot of languages today still have numerous Latin words. In English, for example, the following words come from Latin:

actor (Latin *actor*)
family (Latin *familia*)
second (Latin *secundus*)

You will find lots of Latin words in this book.

You will be able to see when the Romans took over more and more of the Mediterranean world when you turn to the next page and look at the timeline.

RICUM

PANNONIA

DACIA

BLACK SEA

DANMATIA

MOESIA SUPERIOR

MOESIA INFERIOR

THRACIA

BITHYINA AND PONTUS

CAPPADOCIA

Rome

MACEDONIA

GALATIA

ITALIA

ASIA

SYRIA

EPIRUS

LYCIA AND PAMPHYLIA

CILICIA

Corinthus

ACHAEA

CYPRUS

SICILIA

CRETA

JUDAEA

MEDITERRANEAN SEA

ALEXANDRIA

ARABIA

CYRENAICA

AEGYPTUS

TIMELINE

	800–400	400–300	300–200	200–100	100–0
ROME	**753** Legend says Rome was founded by Romulus **509** Romans throw out Etruscan kings Republic established		**264–241** Wars with Carthaginians **237–202** Wars with Carthaginians	**149–146** Wars with Carthaginians Early coin showing Romulus and Remus and the wolf	**83–82** Civil Wars **49–45** Civil Wars **31–29** Civil Wars **44** Julius Caesar becomes "Dictator for Life". Murdered same year
EMPERORS AND EMPIRE			Augustus		**27** Augustus becomes first emperor
CONQUESTS	Standard bearer			**146** North Africa and Greece taken	**59–49** Julius Caesar conquered Gaul and invaded Britain twice Portrait of a Gaul
EVENTS AROUND THE WORLD	**800** First writing used in Americas. **770** Beginning of the Chou Dynasty in China. **521** Darius the Great rules Persian Empire. **500** First copper used in Africa.	**400** Carthage controls the western Mediterranean. **350** Crossbow invented in China.	**300** Mayan civilisation established, **250** Mauryan Empire in India. **240** Parthian Empire established. **221** China unified under Chin Dynasty, Great Wall built.	River boat loading with grain	**50** Chinese silk imported into Rome.

10

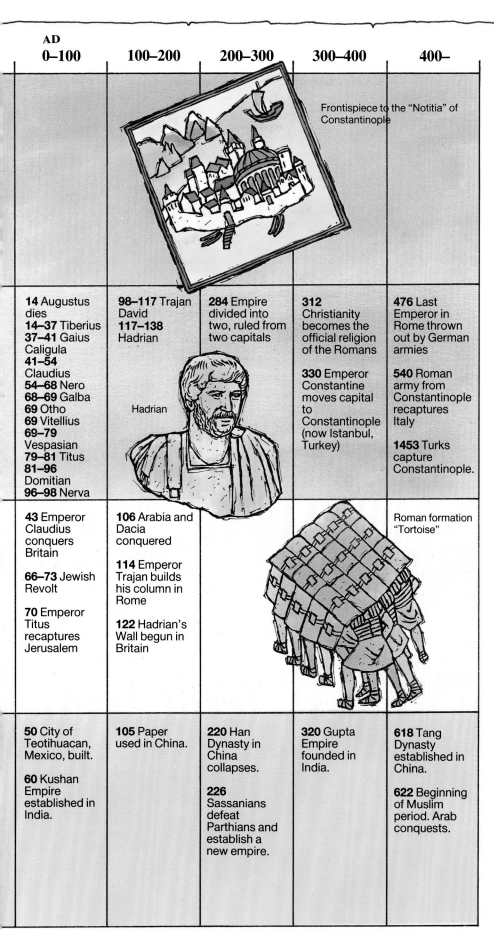

AD 0–100	100–200	200–300	300–400	400–
			Frontispiece to the "Notitia" of Constantinople	
14 Augustus dies **14–37** Tiberius **37–41** Gaius Caligula **41–54** Claudius **54–68** Nero **68–69** Galba **69** Otho **69** Vitellius **69–79** Vespasian **79–81** Titus **81–96** Domitian **96–98** Nerva	**98–117** Trajan David **117–138** Hadrian Hadrian	**284** Empire divided into two, ruled from two capitals	**312** Christianity becomes the official religion of the Romans **330** Emperor Constantine moves capital to Constantinople (now Istanbul, Turkey)	**476** Last Emperor in Rome thrown out by German armies **540** Roman army from Constantinople recaptures Italy **1453** Turks capture Constantinople.
43 Emperor Claudius conquers Britain **66–73** Jewish Revolt **70** Emperor Titus recaptures Jerusalem	**106** Arabia and Dacia conquered **114** Emperor Trajan builds his column in Rome **122** Hadrian's Wall begun in Britain		Roman formation "Tortoise"	
50 City of Teotihuacan, Mexico, built. **60** Kushan Empire established in India.	**105** Paper used in China.	**220** Han Dynasty in China collapses. **226** Sassanians defeat Parthians and establish a new empire.	**320** Gupta Empire founded in India.	**618** Tang Dynasty established in China. **622** Beginning of Muslim period. Arab conquests.

THE LEGEND OF ROME

Roman boys and girls were told a legend about the foundation of Rome. Romulus and Remus, who were twins, were cast adrift in a basket on the River Tiber by their wicked uncle. He hoped they would die but they were rescued by a she-wolf who heard their cries. She suckled the babies. When they grew into boys they were taken in by the royal shepherd, Faustulus, and his wife. Discovering who they really were, they went on to found the city of Rome. The two young brothers argued with each other about who should be king and Romulus killed Remus. Romulus became the first king of Rome in 753 BC.

BC or AD?

Our dates are taken from the year Christ was born. The letters AD stand for *Anno Domini* which means "in the year of the Lord". The years before Christ (BC) are counted backwards. The Romans worked out their yearly dates either from the date of the foundation of Rome or from the list of the consuls elected each year.

WHO·GREW ·THE· ROMANS' ·FOOD?

The Roman Empire could not have become as large as it did and have fed its 60 million inhabitants without farms. In many of the provinces created by the Romans, farming people hardly changed their way of life. But some farmers were able to sell their produce more widely than before. The farmers in Egypt, for instance, produced most of the wheat needed to make bread in the city of Rome.

A NEW PLOW
The plow shown below is a new type which the Romans developed. It turned the soil over. Normally a pair of oxen would pull the plow.

Antler rake

Rake

Iron scythe

Plow

HARVESTING MACHINE
Of course the Romans had no powered machinery, like tractors. But they did invent machines, such as the *vallus* shown below in a sculpture. This harvesting device for crops like wheat and barley was pushed by a donkey or mule. It had wide blades at the front which cut the crop and pushed it into the hopper behind.

COUNTRY ESTATES

Owners of big farming estates often built themselves a central group of buildings known as a *villa*. There would be the farmer's house, a house for his manager, sleeping quarters for the slaves, storehouses and stables. A wall kept out the wild animals and prevented slaves from escaping.

HUNTING WILD BOAR

Hunting played an important part in the Roman diet. It could provide very different types of food, such as the wild boar shown here.

Some Roman crops:
Wheat
Barley
Rye
Oats
Rice

Olives, grapes
(for wine and
for eating), and nuts

Apples
Figs
Cherries
Peaches
Pears
Plums

Carrots
Lettuces
Cabbages
Parsnips
Peas
Radishes
Turnips

All sorts of herbs

Animals the Romans ate:
Cattle
Sheep
Pigs
Goats
Chickens
Pigeons
Geese

Working animals:
Oxen
Cows
Horses
Donkeys
Mules
Camels
Dogs

Ordinary Romans in big towns and cities all over the empire lived in apartments or in rooms above shops. Some of them did their cooking over a fire in a metal frame, known today as a brazier. But most of these buildings were made of wood and there were often serious fires. Various emperors declared that cooking in apartments was illegal. People had to go out to eat, or buy take-away food. They bought from street vendors – salt, sausages and peas pudding were on sale in Rome.

TAKE-AWAY FOOD SHOP
You are looking at a take-away bar and restaurant in the harbor city of Ostia, near Rome. It looks out over a street that once teamed with townspeople, traders and seafarers. There are benches where customers could sit to eat a simple snack, or you could go inside, past the counter, to have a meal. The paintings on the wall advertised what was on the menu – green olives, turnips, eggs, cheese and watermelon. You could drink hot, sweet spiced wine or honey water. A huge storage jar held over 200 gallons of wine.

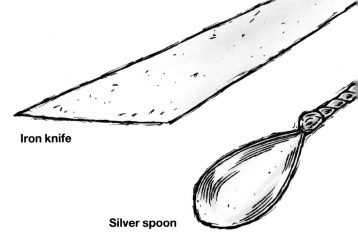

Iron knife

Silver spoon

Bone spatula

Bronze spoon

If you were rich enough to have a house with a kitchen and slaves to do the cooking, you could eat a great variety of foods.

The Romans liked lots of flavors in their dishes. They used herbs and spices such as coriander, oregano, fennel, mint, thyme, sage, nutmeg, cardamom, cumin, pepper and ginger. They loved sauces, especially *liquamen*, made from salted fish and fish insides.

Here are two Roman recipes:

Cabbages with leeks
"Put the boiled cabbages into a shallow saucepan and season wth liquamen, oil, ordinary wine and cumin. Sprinkle with pepper, leeks, caraway seeds and fresh coriander."

Home-made sweets
"Stuffed dates: Take the stones out of the dates and stuff with nuts, pine kernels or ground pepper. Roll them in salt and fry in warmed honey".

POTS AND PANS

Roman take-away bars and homes had a variety of cooking and storage pots. Most were made of clay, like these ones.

SOME ROMAN WORDS

HOW DO WE KNOW?

There are two sorts of evidence about the Roman diet. The Romans themselves wrote recipe books, and food is sometimes mentioned in other writing. Also, archaeologists have carefully excavated places like Ostia and have discovered the remains of things used to cook with and even some of the food itself inside the old Roman buildings.

amphora two-handled container for wine, olive oil or fish sauce
cena dinner
ientaculum breakfast
mortarium mortar for grinding food or spices
popina take-away and restaurant
prandium lunch
triclinium dining room

DID · THE ROMANS · HAVE · FAMILIES LIKE · OURS?

Our word family comes from the Latin word *familia*. But to the Romans it meant more than our idea of a family. *Familia* really means household because it included the slaves which were owned by the head of the family – the father. The slaves served the family and were not free to leave it. Roman law gave the man complete authority over all the members of the *familia*. With this authority came a duty towards them. The head of the family was also the family priest, making offerings to the gods on behalf of them all. Women were not allowed to take part in public life at all.

WEDDING

It was usual for a girl of twelve and a boy of fourteen to be formally engaged after negotiations between their parents. The marriage usually took place several years later. The Romans were very superstitious and believed that the luckiest time to get married was during the second half of June. The marriage ceremony usually took place at the girl's home with the guests shouting out "Good luck!" and throwing nuts to the children. The husband then took his new wife to their own home and carried her over the threshold.

CHILDREN

A boy was considered to be of more use than a girl in the family. Quite often new-born girls were abandoned so that they would be sure to die. Various emperors introduced allowances for poor families to help them bring up their children.

A boy at the age of sixteen was considered to be a man. He had worn a good luck charm, called a *bulla* round his neck since he was a baby. He dedicated it at a special ceremony to the household gods.

A girl dedicated her toys to the household gods when she got married.

A large household always included slaves. They came under the charge of the woman of the house. How well they were treated depended on what sort of people the man and woman were. We do know that many slaves were treated well. Owners of house slaves often left a will which directed that they should be freed.

A slave who was freed did not become a full citizen like those born free. But their children did have full rights.

liberta a freed woman
libertus a freed man

Figurines

Game board

Marbles

Knucklebone

Dice

TOYS

Roman children played with toys. Babies had rattles and squeaky animals. Little figurines were popular. Those shown above were found in the grave of a child who once lived in the Roman town of Colchester in southern Britain. Two of the figures are reading from scrolls and one is reclining as if he were resting on a couch. Perhaps they represent a scene in a house after dinner when readings of poetry sometimes took place. What do you think?

Everyone seemed to play board games in the Roman world. The game board shown above right was found on Hadrian's Wall, a fortified wall built across the north of England to keep out the fierce tribes of northern Britain.

BEWARE OF THE DOG!

The Romans kept pets – mainly dogs and cats – as we do today. Favorite names for dogs were *Celer* (Swift) and *Ferox* (Fierce).

DID·THE ROMANS LIVE·IN HOUSES?

Many Roman families lived in their own houses, just as some people do today. But most of the population of a town, especially if it was a big town, lived in apartments or rooms which they rented. Where you lived depended on what you could afford. Archaeologists have discovered the remains of many sorts of dwellings and their furniture.

A VIEW IN POMPEII
This view is of a typical street in the Roman town of Pompeii in southern Italy. People who had private houses here liked to be as private as possible. There were no front gardens or windows to stare into. Visitors entered through a gate in the front wall.

18

A GARDEN WALK

Right at the back of this house (whose plan is shown below) lies an enclosed garden. The columns hold up a little roof which gives a shaded passage where people could walk out of the hot Italian sun. This is the view the family and their guests would have had from the dining room. The little garden was laid out with statues and beds for flowers and shrubs – perhaps one provided bay leaves for the kitchen.

APARTMENTS AND ROOMS

Most towns and cities were divided into regular blocks by streets and alleyways. Apartment blocks and shops filled these areas. In Rome the apartment buildings were five or six stories high, but elsewhere they reached only two or three stories. Shopkeepers and workshop owners usually lived above their workplace. Accommodation in these flats would have been cramped (unlike the House of the Vettii, far right).

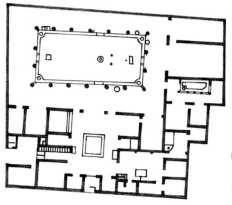

Here is a bird's eye view of the plan of a house of a wealthy person in Pompeii.

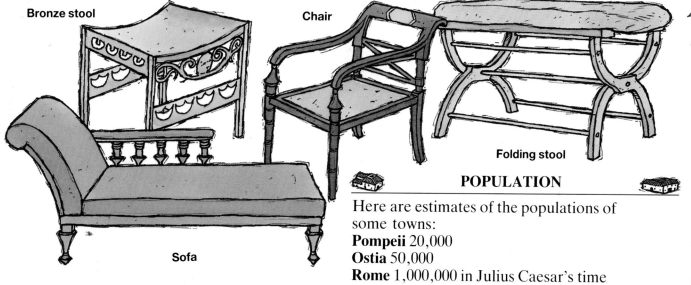

Bronze stool

Chair

Folding stool

Sofa

POPULATION

Here are estimates of the populations of some towns:
Pompeii 20,000
Ostia 50,000
Rome 1,000,000 in Julius Caesar's time

DID·BOYS AND·GIRLS GO·TO SCHOOL?

In the early days of Rome the children of wealthier families were educated at home by private tutors. The father took charge of teaching outdoor skills such as horse-riding, swimming and fighting with weapons and armor. These skills were considered important for the boys. Girls were taught by their mothers how to look after a home and manage the house slaves. Then the idea of schools was introduced and boys and girls could attend a school if their parents could afford the fee to the teachers.

AT SCHOOL

The sculpture below sets the scene in a Roman school where two pupils are seated beside their teacher. They had no desks but read from scrolls or wrote on their wax tablets with a sharp point. These tablets could be erased easily and used many times over. Boys are pictured here because very few girls were sent to school. It was generally considered unnecessary for girls to be educated in this way. Schoolmasters were very strict and were not afraid to use a cane or strap on their pupils to make them learn or behave well.

School began at dawn but was finished by early afternoon. A Roman working week was eight days long – seven working days and one for market day.

Children could expect days off for religious festivals and a long summer holiday from the end of July to the middle of October.

Scrolls

PEN AND INK

There were several means of writing in Roman times. Pen and ink could be used on papyrus which was made into scrolls. Papyrus was made from the flattened leaves of a water plant found mainly in Egypt. Very thin layers of wood were also used like paper to write on. The wax tablet with its layer of wax encased in wood could be used and reused to write everyday notes and lists. Here is a Roman inkpot and pen. The inkpot would originally have had a hinged lid.

WAX TABLETS

The portrait below shows a young Roman woman. Can you see that she is holding two hinged wax tablets in one hand and her writing instrument in the other?

PRIMARY SCHOOL

Pupils began their first school at the age of seven. A schoolmaster would set up a school in his house or in a rented room. The main lessons were reading, writing and arithmetic.

SECONDARY SCHOOL

At the age of eleven pupils read the works of famous Greek and Roman writers and poets. Subjects included history, arithmetic and geometry and sometimes music and athletics.

 EDUCATION

Some pupils went on to higher education. They were almost always young men. At the age of sixteen, a young man who wanted a career as a lawyer or politician went to special tutors. This usually meant travelling to the provinces. Athens and Asia Minor (now called Turkey) were favorite places.

A primary school teacher was paid the same *each month* as a carpenter or wall painter was paid *each day*!

A wax tablet was called a *cera* (literally meaning wax) or *tabula* and the writing instrument was called a *stylus*.

· W H O · WENT·TO WORK·IN ROMAN TIMES ?

Roman towns did not have huge office blocks but people went to work in small businesses, shops and factories. Each of these sorts of work usually involved a family with slaves as well as free apprentices.

The complicated life of the Romans in their huge empire could not work without businesses. There is a good example from Ostia which was the port of Rome. The main business of the town was to see to the import and export of goods by sea. In one of the main squares there were the offices of about 70 firms – ship repairers, timber merchants and ropemakers for example.

THE WORKSHOP

The word factory usually means a huge building with many workers. In Roman times things were manufactured and sold, but it was on a much smaller scale. The word workshop is more appropriate. There were areas in towns which were given over to workshops and within them were whole streets devoted to one particular trade, such as carpentry.

Two craftsmen are shown here in their workshops. On the left is a shoemaker with a selection of sandals on top of his cupboard. On the right is a ropemaker. He is twisting the thread with his right hand. Both these products would have been sold from the workshop.

A BUTCHER'S SHOP

There were no Roman supermarkets but there were plenty of different sorts of shops. Here is a butcher at work facing right onto the street. Most shops were family-run businesses where the product sold (such as bread or cloth) was made on the premises.

IVNIVS

The objects shown on this page relate to many Roman trades.

Some of the trades recorded at Ostia were:
carpenters
clothmakers
painters
bakers
ferrymen
fur traders
fishermen
fishmongers

Civil servants included:
wax tablet clerks
messengers
weights and measures clerks

Merchants included:
bankers
oil merchants
grain merchants
wine importers

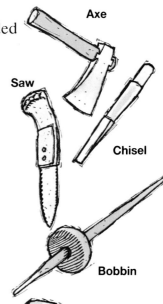

Axe

Saw

Chisel

Bobbin

THE SLAVE TRADE

No Roman industry could work without slaves. Large industries such as mining and farming used huge numbers of slaves. There were few small businesses and shops that did not own slaves. Some were treated very harshly by their owners. If they ran away, slaves were branded with a red-hot iron when they were caught. The mosaic shown here, from the town of Pompeii, pictures a slave boy who worked in the house of a rich family. A household slave was often treated like one of the family.

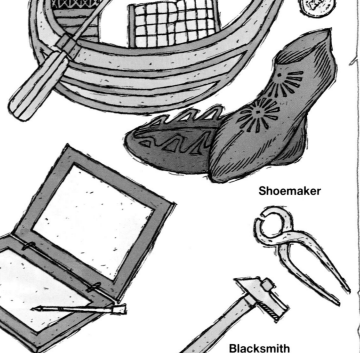

Ferryman

Shoemaker

Weights and measures

Wax tablet

Blacksmith

23

· W H A T ·
D I D · T H E
R O M A N S
D O · O N
· T H E I R ·
H O L I D A Y S ?

The Romans did not really go on vacation as we do today. The rich people who lived in towns might have a number of houses on their farming estates. A popular place for vacation homes for those who lived in Rome was at the seaside around the Bay of Naples. For the ordinary working family there were a very large number of religious festival days scattered throughout the year. On these days Romans could choose from a variety of entertainments.

FIGHTS TO THE DEATH

The favorite entertainment for most people was to go to the amphitheater to watch fights to the death. Trained men called gladiators were set against each other. Gladiators were usually slaves who had been captured in war. The Romans also imported large numbers of wild animals and set up animal hunts. Gladiators, criminals or persecuted minorities like Jews or Christians were forced to fight against animals like lions, tigers, bears, hyenas and even rhinos.

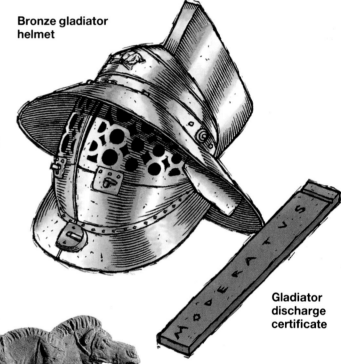

Bronze gladiator helmet

Gladiator discharge certificate

CHARIOT RACING

Huge numbers of excited people went to see chariot racing. The races were very dangerous and people liked to bet on the results. Many towns had their own stadium, but Rome had the biggest of all. The chariots pulled by four horses were in four teams. The charioteers wore the colors of their teams which were called the Reds, the Blues, the Greens and the Whites.

GLADIATORS

CHARIOTEERS

Retiarius Man armed with a net and three-pronged spear. He fought a *secutor* armed with a sword and shield.
Thracian Man armed with a round shield and curved sword.
Mirmillo and *Samnite* Heavily armed men carrying oblong shields and short swords. They wore helmets with visors.

Some astounding figures for capacity audiences:
50,000 in the Colosseum, Rome's main amphitheater.
20,000 in the amphitheater in Pompeii.

Rome's chariot racing circus was called the Circus Maximus. It held:
100,000 people, first century BC.
250,000 people, first century AD.
350,000 people, fourth century AD.

Diocles was a very famous charioteer. He drove chariots for 24 years, entered 4,257 races and won 1,462 races.

ROMAN BATHS

The bath house was a favorite place to go every day for a chat, to conduct business, to meet friends, to play dice games, to have a snack – and to go through a complicated set of bathing pools. This is the Great Bath in the Roman town of Aquae Sulis (now Bath) in Britain. Before the Romans went in here they would have gone through a warm steamy room, a very hot steamy room, a hot dip bath and had a massage. To finish off they went for a cold dip and some exercise.

Flask for hot oil

Two *strigils* (body scrapers)

Roman clothes were not at all like the ones people wear in western countries today. They were loose fitting and suitable for the hot Mediterranean climate. The tunic was the garment most commonly worn by men, women and children. Only men who were Roman citizens could wear the *toga*. Working people wore simpler clothes made from coarser materials. Underpants were a piece of cloth tied round your waist like a loincloth. Women wore a kind of bra as well, although it was more like a breast band. All people wore sandals.

ROMAN COSTUME
This Roman statesman wears the *toga*, the national dress for Roman men. They wore it over their tunics. The *toga* was a semicircular piece of cloth just over 18 feet long which had to be carefully draped around the body from the shoulders. In cold weather it could be pulled over the head. The *toga* for citizens had to be pure white. The *toga* probably came to be used on formal occasions only.

HAIR AND CLOTHES
The sculpture above gives you a good idea of some women's clothes. Here the lady of the house is sitting in a basket chair having her hair done by her house slaves. One is holding a mirror for her. The lady is wearing a dress called a *stola* which reaches to her ankles. This shows that she is married. Under her dress she would be wearing at least one long tunic. The slave girls are just wearing simple tunics.

Tunics and *stolas* were made from wool, linen or silk in a variety of colors – white, black, green, blue, yellow, red or purple.

HOW TO WEAR YOUR TOGA
The *toga* (1) was semi-circular – its width was three times the height of the person. Drape over left shoulder (2) and pass the other end (3) under arm and across shoulder.

WORKING CLOTHES

Most working people wore the tunic, but some Romans adopted the idea of trousers, called *bracae*. These were skin tight and stretched down to the ankles. They were popular with soldiers serving in Britain and Germany, as they provided protection from cold weather. Outside workers, like farmers, often wore a woollen overcoat with a hood. People also wore knitted socks and stockings.

Brooch

Necklace

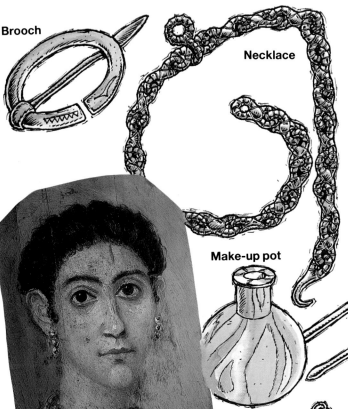

Make-up pot

In early Roman times women had simple hairstyles – often just a bun held at the back of the head with pins or with a hairnet called a *reticulum*. In the times of the emperors elaborate hairstyles like these shown here became popular. Wigs were available if you could afford it. The hair came from blonde women captured in Germany or from dark-haired Indian girls.

Fashionable men wore their hair combed forward. Sometimes they had it curled. Most men were clean shaven up to the second century AD. After that beards became the fashion.

Scent bottle

Spatula for make-up

Armband

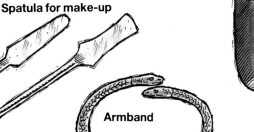

Earrings

Toga

Stola

A LADY OF FASHION

We have this picture of a rich Roman lady from Egypt because her portrait was painted on her coffin. Roman ladies liked earrings and necklaces. Make-up consisted of chalk for a fashionable white skin, red ochre to color cheeks and for lipstick, and ash for darkening eyebrows. You could buy sets of little instruments hanging from a ring for plucking eyebrows and cleaning out your ears!

SOME ROMAN WORDS

subligaculum underpants or loincloth
strophium bra
palla very large shawl worn by women for the cold outdoors

WHO·DID·THE·ROMANS·WORSHIP?

The Romans believed in the existence of many gods and spirits who controlled everything they did. It was important to try to make them friendly. They thought spirits could be anywhere – in trees or streams or in the ground. The Romans imagined their gods and goddesses in human form but usually bigger and certainly more powerful. They took some gods from the ancient Greeks and gave them new names. Others they adopted from countries they conquered. They even made their emperors into gods after they had died.

HOUSE FOR A GOD

The Romans did not go to their temples in the same way that people today might go to a church, mosque or synagogue. The temple was the house for a particular god or goddess. This was where their statue was and where the priests or priestesses carried out ceremonies or made sacrifices or offerings to them. The Romans made vows, or promises, to a favorite god or goddess in exchange for their help. The temple shown below was built in 16 BC at the Roman town of Nemausus (Nîmes) in the south of France. The temple was dedicated to Rome and the Emperor Augustus and is one of the best surviving temples.

THE GODDESS DIANA

This statue shows the way in which the Romans pictured a goddess. Diana was a goddess of women and of the hunt. Offerings would be made to her when a woman was to give birth.

Apollo

Mithras

Hercules

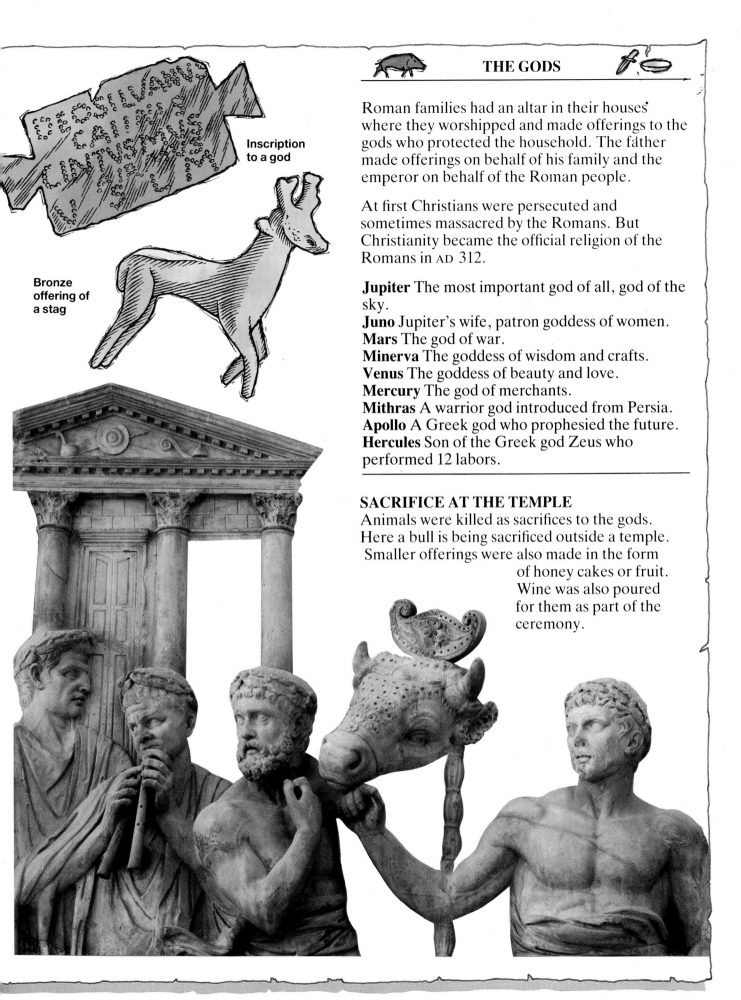

Inscription to a god

Bronze offering of a stag

Roman families had an altar in their houses where they worshipped and made offerings to the gods who protected the household. The father made offerings on behalf of his family and the emperor on behalf of the Roman people.

At first Christians were persecuted and sometimes massacred by the Romans. But Christianity became the official religion of the Romans in AD 312.

Jupiter The most important god of all, god of the sky.
Juno Jupiter's wife, patron goddess of women.
Mars The god of war.
Minerva The goddess of wisdom and crafts.
Venus The goddess of beauty and love.
Mercury The god of merchants.
Mithras A warrior god introduced from Persia.
Apollo A Greek god who prophesied the future.
Hercules Son of the Greek god Zeus who performed 12 labors.

SACRIFICE AT THE TEMPLE

Animals were killed as sacrifices to the gods. Here a bull is being sacrificed outside a temple. Smaller offerings were also made in the form of honey cakes or fruit. Wine was also poured for them as part of the ceremony.

DID·THE ROMANS GO·TO·THE DOCTOR?

The Romans worshipped a god of healing called Aesculapius. But they also had doctors who were introduced into Italy from Greece. We know of Roman men and women doctors, as well as eye specialists and midwives to help with childbirth. Towns could employ doctors for the community and give them a salary. A small town was allowed five doctors by law. Hospitals and clinics were mostly based in private houses – in one house in Pompeii many medical instruments were found.

AT THE DOCTOR'S

Doctors used many different sorts of treatments for illness. For example, hot mashed turnips were used as a cure for chilblains and mustard for stomach upsets. The instruments used included needles for sewing wounds, forceps and clamps. Round containers were used for drugs. The doctor in the sculpture is treating a female patient for an eye complaint. Pharmacists sold blocks of different ointments for eye complaints such as inflammation. The stamp shown was used to print the name of the supplier and the drug onto the block. The name Titus

Ointment stamp

Vindacius Ariovistus, is cut (in mirror writing) along with a selection of ointment names. When the stamp was pressed onto the ointment the letters could be read the right way round.

SURGERY

Doctors were able to treat some very serious illnesses, though they had none of the the high technology instruments that hospitals have today. Roman doctors cut into the skull to relieve pressure on the brain, and they were able to make artificial limbs and false teeth.

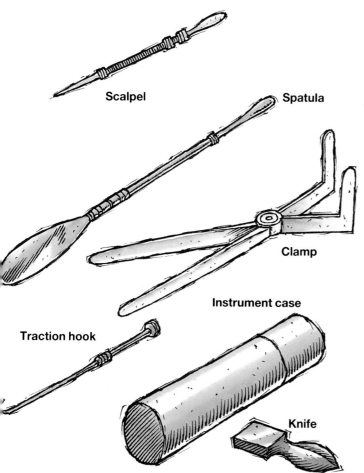

Scalpel

Spatula

Clamp

Traction hook

Instrument case

Knife

Sometimes great epidemics killed off large numbers of people. During the reign of the Emperor Nero, 30,000 people died of some kind of plague, in AD 65. The average age of death in Roman times was between 35 and 50. Poor people would rarely survive over the age of 50.

Roman law stated that people must be buried outside the town's walls. Cemeteries usually lined the roads into the town. The tombstone shown here was for Curatia Dinysia. She was 40 when she died in Chester, England.

Some Roman words:
medicus doctor
valetudinarium hospital

BURIAL

Tombstones and *mausolea* (houses for the dead) were put up for those who could afford them in cemeteries outside towns. The sarcophagus shown below has a carving of the scene of a girl's death. She is laid out on a couch while her little dog sits underneath near her sandals. The women around are professional mourners – paid to weep and wail during the procession to the tomb. The girl's father and mother sit sadly on either side.

· WHO · RULED · ROME? ·

During the Roman period the people had different forms of government. First they had kings, but they were hated and were soon thrown out. In their place they invented the republic, a form of government in which the people voted in their own rulers. Officials usually held power for one or two years. Gradually, ambitious men wanted more power for themselves. The republic was replaced by the rule of an all-powerful king they called emperor.

THE SENATORS

During the rule of the republic there was a sort of parliament called the senate which was made up of elders who had served in the government. The senate discussed important matters of state and gave advice to the officials of the government. The men in the stately group shown below are all senators. Notice that they are wearing the *toga*. Governors were appointed for each province outside Italy, but individual towns had their own elected council.

EMPEROR HADRIAN

The Emperor Hadrian ruled the Roman world from AD 177 to AD 138. He was born in Spain. He served in the army and held various posts under the previous emperor, Trajan, who adopted him as heir to the great empire. Hadrian travelled all through the empire and made sure that Roman people in the provinces were safe from their enemies. He encouraged them to spread the idea of a superior Roman way of life.

All free citizens of the republic had a vote. The main officials were:

Consuls There were two consuls who acted as heads of state and controlled the armed forces.

Praetors Looked after the law courts and the provinces.

Quaestors Dealt with the state's finances.

Censors Kept a register of citizens' names.

Aediles Supervised public works.

Tribunes Looked after the interests of ordinary working people.

Dictator Could be elected for a sixth-month period in a state of emergency. He held absolute power on his own but had an assistant, called a *magister equitum* (master of the horse).

The Roman word for republic was *respublica* which meant "a matter for the people".

Romans were divided into different 'classes':

Patricians Originally the old families of Rome who owned most of the land.

Plebeians The ordinary working people.

Equites The rich business class.

People who were not allowed to vote:
women
children
slaves

Voting was carried out between sunrise and sunset on special days. People were counted and votes were recorded on tablets.

At election time posters were painted onto walls. At Pompeii this slogan can still be seen today:

"If anyone refuses to vote for Quintius let him be carried through the town on the back of a donkey."

An election poster

· W E R E ·
· T H E R E ·
R O M A N
A R T I S T S ?

Plenty of evidence survives today to tell us that the Romans enjoyed art and liked to see it in their private houses and in their public buildings. Compared to modern countries the Romans displayed a large number of statues and other sculptures in their towns. These carvings in stone or bronze were of gods, goddesses, emperors and politicians. A family would also have sculptures of their ancestors in the house. Portraits of the dead were often shown on tombstones (see page 31) for everyone to see.

PAINTINGS AND DECORATIONS

Those Romans who could afford houses liked to have as much of them decorated as possible. Entire walls were painted and ceilings could have complicated painted patterns too. Roman artists also produced small panel paintings to be hung on a wall or to be displayed on an easel. The picture here shows a favorite type – a still life. There is a rabbit, a partridge, an apple and some grapes.

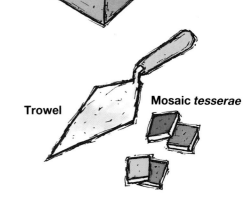

Box for mosaic cubes

Trowel **Mosaic *tesserae***

WALL PAINTINGS

Wall paintings were usually made in the *fresco* technique – the paint was applied before the last skim of plaster had dried.

Favorite colors were:
Red and yellow (from ochre)
White (from chalk)
Green (from green earth)
Black (from soot or carbon)
Blue (from a mixture of glass and copper)
Purple (from a special sea shell called *murex*)

Have you ever seen Roman mosaics in a museum? They are often displayed against a wall. Almost all the ones in museums today were orginally made to cover floors in Roman houses. Each mosaic floor was made from lots of little cubes of stone or tile. These cubes were called *tesserae*. With thousands of small cubes in a large number of different colors, mosaic artists could make their pictures as detailed as a painting.

At Kenchreae, in Greece, Roman wooden crates full of mosaic floors were found on board a ship which had sunk in AD 375.

Mosaics could be made of broken pieces of brick, pottery, stone or glass.

It took about 15 million *tesserae* cubes to lay a floor 50 square feet.

Some small mosaic floors could be bought "ready to lay", stuck onto a piece of canvas.

Julius Caesar was said to have taken small mosaic pictures with him on his campaigns.

FISHERMEN MOSAIC

This mosaic floor picture shows a favorite scene in Roman houses. A fisherman at work with his net off the coast of North Africa. Mosaics like this often show the types of fish caught. In this case it is an octopus – a favorite dish for the Romans.

ARCHITECTURE

All Roman towns had a great variety of public buildings – places for entertainment, for government and for religion. This is the Colosseum, Rome's main amphitheater, which was opened to the public in AD 80. The Romans loved arches and beautifully carved columns.

DID·THE ROMANS GO·TO ·THE· THEATER?

Romans all over the empire went to the theater to see plays, mimes and concerts. By the fourth century AD, theaters in Rome were open on 100 days in the year. The Romans developed some kinds of theater entertainment themselves but the idea of proper plays came from the Greeks.

There were two sorts of Greek play – tragedies (serious plays) and comedies. Roman playwrights also made up their own sorts of plays – slapstick comedies with clowns about life in the country, comedies based on village characters, or tragedies on historical themes.

ACTORS

The mosaics below once decorated a house in Pompeii. It shows actors getting ready for a performance. You can see one of the men putting his costume on and a musician rehearsing on the pipes. The strange heads are masks which helped the actors to throw their voices in the huge auditorium. Boldly painted masks also helped the audience to identify the sort of character being played.

Lituus
An instrument used for funeral processions and by the army.

Bucina
A trumpet used mainly in the army.

Cithara
A form of lyre. Its strings were plucked.

Cornu
A hoop-like horn used especially for religious processions, funerals and ceremonies. Also used by the army.

Hydraulis
An organ with air forced through the pipes by a water pump. It was used to provide music during fights between gladiators in the amphitheater. It was also used in the theater and sometimes in the home.

MUSIC

Music was an important part of stage performances and people could also go to a concert in a little theatre called an *odeon*. Musicians had the choice of a number of different instruments. Parts of several instruments have survived today (as shown above) but you can also see what they looked like in paintings and mosaics. The double pipes appear in the mosaic picture here.

THE THEATER
A Roman theater looked very much like a Greek theater. People sat in rows which formed a half circle facing the stage. This theater in Orange, in southern France, is one of the best preserved from Roman times. It could hold 20,000 people. Going to the theater was free – all paid for by rich citizens who wanted the audiences to vote for them in local elections!

ENTERTAINMENT
Other musical instruments played by Roman musicians were:
Tuba long trumpet
Tibiae double pipes
Fistula panpipes
Cymbala cymbals
Typanum tambourine

What did they sound like?
. . . not an easy question to answer. Some instruments do survive and can still be played.

At the theater you could see:
Full-length plays
Mimes (*mimus*) Sketches or scenes usually about city life.
Pantomimes (*pantomimus*) A variation on ballet with music.

Actors wore special clothes to help the audience identify the characters:
Wigs were red for slaves, black for young men, white for old men.
Costumes were white for old men, purple for young men, yellow for women.

Men usually played women's parts except in mimes.
Actresses were allowed on the stage in these sketches.

TRAJAN'S COLUMN
The Emperor Trajan built a gigantic column in Rome in AD 114 to commemorate a great military victory. It shows scenes of battles and of life in the army. Here you can see various musical instruments. Instruments were used to sound an advance or retreat in battle as well as for ceremonies. Can you make out what these instruments are?

The Romans were very good at solving problems, and were especially inventive in their building techniques. They needed the skills of surveyors, engineers, architects and builders for many reasons including helping people travel across the empire. They also provided services for people in towns – well-paved streets, a water supply and a sewage system. Buildings such as amphitheatres and circuses were a challenge to design and construct.

CRANES
This wooden crane could help lift huge weights onto buildings. It is worked by a treadmill – men turn the huge wheel at the bottom.

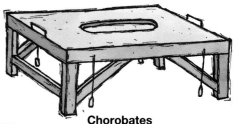

Chorobates

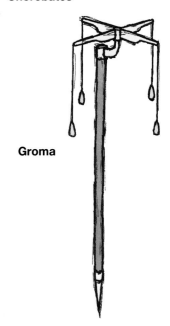

Groma

SURVEYING
The Romans invented special machinery and instruments to help in their building and construction. One Roman invention was the *groma* shown above. Surveyors and architects used it to sight out a straight line and to set lines at right angles by looking through the plumb bobs hanging on strings. The *chorobates* was used like a modern spirit level to get a level surface. The groove in the centre was filled with water.

LAVATORIES

A lot of water was needed for public lavatories. The one shown below is in the town of Ostia. Water was brought by pipe into a channel which ran around the building and under the lavatory seats, providing continuous flushing! The little channel in front of the seats also had water where the Romans dipped sponges to clean themselves. Lavatory paper had not yet been invented. There was usually a lavatory in the baths which might also be open to the public.

AN AQUEDUCT

This stone aqueduct was built in the Roman province of Gaul. Here it carried water in its top channel over a river to the town of Nîmes.

Roman surveyors used the *groma* to measure out land they took over in the provinces as well as to lay out roads. Land was divided into great squares with roads running on each side. This system was called *centuriation*.

Roman roads were not always straight over their whole length. Surveyors used high points to measure out long stretches. Did you know that you can still travel today along routes in Europe which were originally laid out by the Romans?

Some Roman words:
aqua water (Try to find out what the word is in other European languages.)
aqueduct This simply means a way of bringing water. (We still use the word duct today to mean a pipe or channel.)
Find out what the word viaduct means.

DID·THE ROMANS GO·ON ·LONG· JOURNEYS?

Although there were excellent roads which stretched the whole length and breadth of the Roman Empire, few Romans made long journeys. Ordinary working people rarely left their own neighborhood. Soldiers, however, traveled vast distances across the empire, as did governors of provinces and several emperors. The people who traveled most regularly were the merchants who carried goods by sea and by land, even from beyond the borders of the empire. Many goods were carried by camel trains from the East. The Romans traded with foreigners outside the empire but thought they were "barbarians".

MILESTONES ON THE ROAD

The Romans laid solid roads throughout the empire. As provinces were taken over, the army was responsible for building new roads. The civilian authorities then had to maintain them and build new ones as they were needed. The road below with its milestone is at Carthage in north Africa. The milestone recorded distances to important settlements.

TRAVEL BY SEA

Most goods were transported by ship wherever possible. The main port of Rome, Ostia, was gradually enlarged to cope with this trade; the Emperors Claudius and Trajan constructed great harbors there. Ships like the ones below carried great pottery jars called *amphorae*, full of wine, olive oil or fish sauce. A ship might carry 6,000 *amphorae*. They were specially shaped so that they could be stowed on board ship.

Along the main routes the Romans established an offical courier system to carry mail and safeguard people traveling on government business. It was called the *cursus publicus*. Government hotels called *mansiones* could be used by officials.

Some of the goods traded:
From Britain – hunting dogs, woollen cloaks, silver, lead
From Spain – fish sauce, wine, olive oil, cloth
From Egypt – papyrus, corn
From Gaul (France) – wine, pottery
From Greece – wine, marble, purple dye
From the East and China – silks, spices, perfumes, jewels

A merchant ship might travel 100 miles a day.

A camel train could cover about 21 miles a day.

The official post, with frequent changes of horses, could travel about 43 miles in a day.

TRAVEL BY CART

Roman roads may have provided good routes for the army and for goods but they were unpleasant to travel along. Long distances could be covered in horse-drawn carriages (rather like stagecoaches) like the ones shown below. It was bumpy and dirty for passengers, as well as slow.

WHAT·WAS LIFE·LIKE IN·THE ROMAN ·ARMY?·

You had to be tough to be a Roman soldier. Your chances of being wounded or killed were much greater than in most armies nowadays. Soldiers were used to conquering new lands, policing the provinces and putting down rebellions. In a population of about 60 million, the Roman Empire had about 450,000 soldiers. Once a soldier had joined up he had to go through rigorous, and often dangerous, training. In enemy territory the army would build a camp each evening. It was fortified with an earth wall and wooden fence. There were permanent stone-built forts on frontiers like Hadrian's Wall.

ARMY LIFE

The carving below comes from Trajan's Column in Rome (see page 37). It shows his campaigns in Dacia, north of the River Danube. Here you can see in detail what life was like in the Roman army. Soldiers are in the thick of battle, advancing in boats and crossing a ford.

A Roman soldier would be expected to march all day in full armor, with spear, shield, sword and dagger, and carrying equipment on his back weighing 66 lbs. A soldier's equipment included a saw, basket, pick, axe, strap, bill-hook, chain and three days' rations.

A CAVALRY OFFICER

This rider, Titus Flavius Bassus, was 41 years old when he died. He was a cavalry officer and his tombstone shows him riding down an enemy 'barbarian'. A servant in the background brings him other weapons.

THE ROMAN SOLDIER

A Roman soldier served 20 years on average.

Out of his basic pay a soldier had to pay for his food, clothes and weapons.

There was a Roman navy though it was not considered to be as important as the army. Roman seamen served for 26 years either as rowers or marines. A typical warship had 300 rowers and 120 marines.

Some army words:
Testudo The formation Roman soldiers made with their shields held over their heads and on all sides as a protection against missiles.
Ballista An artillery machine which fired short bolts with iron tips.

OFFICERS AND MEN

Soldiers joined up as *legionaries* – they were assigned to a *legion* of about 5,600 men. Legions were divided into smaller units called *cohorts* but they trained, lived and fought in *centuriae* (this means groups of a hundred men) commanded by a *centurion*. A centurion was equivalent to a sergeant in a modern army. The legion's commander, called a *legatus*, had officers to help him. They were called *tribunes* and usually served a short time as part of a career in politics.

LETTERS HOME

Did Roman soldiers write letters home? We know they did because various letters have survived. This picture of a fragment shows

part of a note from Vindolanda, a fort on Hadrian's Wall in northern Britain. One soldier's mother sent this note (not all of it survives) with a parcel:

"I have sent you . . . pairs of wollen socks, two pairs of sandals and two pairs of underpants . . ."

A ROMAN LEGIONARY

This is how a Roman legionary soldier was armed. The upper part of his body was protected by metal armor. His special helmet stopped blows from the swords of his enemies cutting his neck. The large curved shield protected him from attack. After throwing their spears the legionaries would march in formation against the enemy cutting and stabbing with their short swords.

· GLOSSARY ·

AMPHITHEATER Oval arena where gladiators fought each other or wild animals. The word means "theater in the round". The Colosseum is Rome's most famous amphitheater.

AQUEDUCT Channel bringing water into the cities. Many aqueducts were built of stone, but some were just water courses cut into the ground.

ARCHAEOLOGY Study of the remains of the past – objects or structures under the ground or sea, on the surface or in standing buildings.

CARTHAGE The capital city of Rome's most dangerous enemy – the Carthaginians. Hannibal was the Carthaginian general who led his army, with elephants, across the Alps into Italy.

CENTURION Soldier in charge of 100 men.

CHARIOTEER Driver of four-horse chariots in the circus. Chariot-racing was a very skilled but dangerous profession.

CIRCUS Arena where chariot races were held.

COHORTS Units of a Roman legion.

EMPEROR Held supreme power in the state.

FAMILIA Household including family and slaves.

GLADIATORS Warriors who fought to the death. Most were slaves but some actually chose to become gladiators!

HADRIAN Emperor famous for his 'wall' across Britain and for his developing towns right across the empire. Probably the most traveled emperor.

LATIN Language spoken and written by the Romans.

LEGION Division of the Roman army of about 5,500 men.

LIQUAMEN Strong fish sauce used in cooking. It was transported in great pottery jars called *amphorae* and was added to most Roman dishes.

MAUSOLEUM Large tomb to hold coffin or ashes of the dead.

ODEON Small theater used for concerts.

PAPYRUS 'Paper' made from leaves of a water plant. Egypt was the most important producer of papyrus. 'Books' were handwritten on papyrus scrolls.

PATRICIANS Upper class of Roman society.

PLEBEIANS Name given to working people.

REPUBLIC Roman state with elected officials.

SENATE A body that discussed government affairs. Senators had all served as officials in government at some time.

TRIBUNE Officer in a Roman legion.

WAX TABLETS Used to write notes on. Some tablets have survived with the marks of writing on the wooden outside. The wax has disappeared.

ROMAN MONTHS	
Januarius	January
Februarius	February
Martius	March
Aprilis	April
Maius	May
Junius	June
Julius	July (named after Julius Caesar); originally called Quintilis
Augustus	August (named after the Emperor Augustus); originally called Sextilis
September	September
October	October
December	December

Julius Caesar reorganized the calendar. He declared that there would be 365 days in the year but added an extra day to February every fourth year – our Leap Year. This new calendar, called the Julian Calendar after Julius Caesar, began on 1 January 45 BC.

ROMAN NUMBERS
I 1
II 2
III 3
IIII or IV 4
V 5
VI 6
VII 7
VIII 8
IX 9
X 10
L 50
C 100
D 500
M 1000

WEIGHTS AND MEASURES
Libra A Roman pound weight 11½ ounces.
Sextarius A measurement for liquid and corn (about ½ quart).
Pes A Roman foot (about 11⅔ inches).
Mille passuum A Roman mile. The words mean a thousand paces (about 9/10 of a mile).

· I N D E X ·